John Rutter

Choral Works

for TTBB choirs

OXFORD

OXFORD
UNIVERSITY PRESS

Great Clarendon Street, Oxford OX2 6DP,
United Kingdom

Oxford University Press is a department of the University of Oxford.
It furthers the University's objective of excellence in research, scholarship,
and education by publishing worldwide. Oxford is a registered trade mark of
Oxford University Press in the UK and in certain other countries

First published 2022

Impression: 1

ISBN 978–0–19–356102–1

Music originated on Sibelius
Printed in Great Britain on acid-free paper by
Halstan & Co. Ltd, Amersham, Bucks.

Contents

A Gaelic Blessing

William Sharp (1855–1905)
adapted by JR

JOHN RUTTER

*The signs ⌐ ¬ denote the melody line, when it is not in the top voice.
The organ accompaniment to the mixed-voice version is compatible with the voice parts of this TTBB version.

Blow, blow, thou winter wind

Words by William Shakespeare

JOHN RUTTER

The original version, for mixed choir, is also published (ISBN 978-0-19-340552-3). The present arrangement is compatible with the composer's orchestration (2 flutes, harp, harpsichord, strings).

man's in-gra-ti - tude,_____ as man's in - gra - ti -

TENORS 1 and 2 A
unis. **mp** *dolce espress.*

Thy tooth is not so keen,_____ Be -

-tude;_____

A

-cause thou art not seen,_____ Al - though thy breath be_

rude,___ al - though thy breath be_ rude._____

* The signs ⌐ ¬ denote the melody line, when it is not in the top voice.

Candlelight Carol

Words and music by
JOHN RUTTER

*If the accompaniment is played on the piano, some notes in the left-hand chords will need to be omitted.
This carol is available in its original version for mixed voices (ISBN 978-019-340738-1) and also for upper voices (978-019-353365-3).

* The signs ⌐ ⌐ denote the melody line, when it is not in the top voice.

*or other vocalized sound, such as 'Oo', at conductor's discretion.

man - ger: Christ our Re - deem - er a - sleep   in the   hay,

God-head in – car-nate and   hope   of sal - va - tion: *Hum*

God-head in – car-nate and   hope   of sal - va - tion: *Hum*

God-head in – car-nate and   hope   of sal - va - tion: A   child with   his

God-head in – car-nate and   hope__   of sal - va - tion: *Hum*

Sw. *p*

Man.

God be in my head

Words from the Sarum Primer (1514)

JOHN RUTTER

*The signs ⌐ ¬ denote the melody line, when it is not in the top voice.

Also available in its original version for mixed voices (ISBN 978-0-19-340551-6).

Lead, kindly Light

Words by John Henry Newman (1801–90)

JOHN RUTTER

Nativity Carol

Words and music by
JOHN RUTTER

* The signs ⌐ ¬ denote the melody line, when it is not in the top voice.

Also available in its original version for mixed voices (ISBN 978-0-19-340571-4).

(Small notes for organ only)

O waly, waly

(The water is wide)

Somerset folk-song
arranged by
JOHN RUTTER

*The original version of this arrangement, for mixed voices, is also published (ISBN 978-0-19-351351-8).

*The solo line from here to the end is shown an octave higher than sounding pitch.

in memoriam Edward T. Chapman

The Lord bless you and keep you

Numbers 6: 24

JOHN RUTTER

Also available in its original version for mixed voices (ISBN 978-0-19-340571-4), and in a two-part version with an accompaniment for piano (ISBN 978-0-19-341521-6).

* The signs ⌐ ¬ denote the melody line, when it is not in the top voice.

When the saints go marching in

American traditional song
arranged by **JOHN RUTTER**

This arrangement is also available in its original version, for mixed voices (ISBN 978-0-19-343151-5).

*Small notes are for rehearsal only. The solo parts are shown an octave higher than sounding pitch.

*Small notes may optionally be taken by a few high tenors.